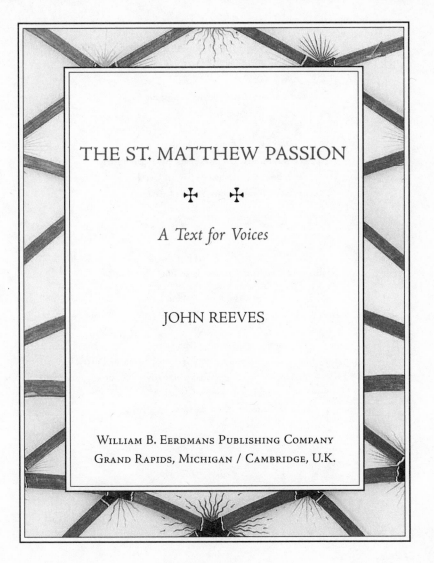

THE ST. MATTHEW PASSION

✠ ✠

A Text for Voices

JOHN REEVES

WILLIAM B. EERDMANS PUBLISHING COMPANY
GRAND RAPIDS, MICHIGAN / CAMBRIDGE, U.K.

© 2001 Wm. B. Eerdmans Publishing Co.

All rights reserved

Wm. B. Eerdmans Publishing Co.

255 Jefferson Ave. S.E., Grand Rapids, Michigan 49503 /

P.O. Box 163, Cambridge CB3 9PU U.K.

Printed in the United States of America

05 04 03 02 01   7 6 5 4 3 2 1

Library of Congress Cataloging-in-Publication Data

Reeves, John, 1926–

The St. Matthew passion: a text for voices / John Reeves.

p.   cm.

ISBN 0-8028-3900-2 (alk. paper)

1. Bach, Johann Sebastian, 1685–1750. Mattheuspassion — Poetry.

2. Jesus Christ — Passion — Poetry. 3. Passion narratives (Gospels) — Poetry.

4. Christian poetry, Canadian.

I. Title: Saint Matthew passion.   II. Title.

PR9199.3.R425 S7 2001

811'.54 — dc21

00-063663

www.eerdmans.com

In Memoriam
Karl Erb
Kathleen Ferrier

Contents

Preface

M usical settings of the story of Christ's Passion, as recounted by
St. Matthew, date back to antiquity. The text was incorporated
early into the liturgy of the Mass for Palm Sunday, and was therefore
chanted by the celebrant. Later, in medieval times, the custom grew up
in monastic churches of having the narrative chanted by one priest, the
words of Jesus by another, and the words of other characters in the
story by various cantors, all to Gregorian chant. In the sixteenth century, composers began to interpolate polyphonic settings of the words
of the crowd, and this initiative led, in the seventeenth century, to more
elaborate settings of the text for choir and soloists with instrumental
accompaniment. The best of these settings, by Heinrich Schütz, is still
widely performed. These earlier settings can be viewed, however, as
simply leading up to J. S. Bach's setting, which is justly considered to be
one of the greatest achievements of Western music. It is also, and not
incidentally, proof of Bach's depth of faith as a devout Christian.

The present cycle of twenty-one verse-meditations is inspired by Bach's masterpiece. The reader should "hear" the text as though uttered by three voices, as indicated by Roman numerals. Voice I speaks for the author, reflecting on his experience of hearing Bach in various cities of the modern world — though the first poem actually deals with the Schütz Passion. Voice II represents, imaginatively, the persona of Bach himself, speaking from the year 1729 when he premiered his St. Matthew Passion in Leipzig, where he was Cantor at the church of St. Thomas, the Thomaskirche. Voice III stands for the whole body of worship in Western Christendom and evokes an earlier period that is sometimes called the "Age of Faith." These poems in the third voice reflect on the place of Christ's Passion in the life of the faithful and on its central role in the liturgy.

The poems are introduced and linked by short passages of prose. These identify the cities visited by the author, annotate Bach's response to the Passion as a believer and composer, and evoke the various liturgies in which the Church has commemorated the Passion. These passages also relate the poems, one by one, to the point reached in the Passion story; and in a few cases they provide translations of German phrases incorporated into the poems.

Appended to the poems is an English translation of Bach's libretto. The narrative and dramatic portions of his text were taken from the Gospel according to St. Matthew in the Lutheran Bible. By way of comment on the story, Bach interpolated traditional Lutheran chorales and reflective poems that he set as recitatives, arias, and choruses.

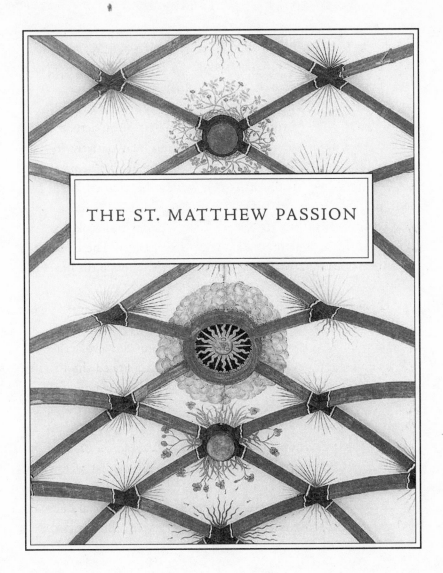

THE ST. MATTHEW PASSION

Visiting Budapest during the later years of the Communist regime, the author became aware of a double life led there: the citizens necessarily displayed an apparent obedience to the dictates of the authorities, but at the same time privately nourished a belief in their own autonomy. This was strikingly manifest in their widespread churchgoing, which they persisted in despite the official atheism of the state. And nowhere was this more evident than in their attendance at Mass on Palm Sunday.

Budapest

❋   ❋

I

These twin cities, long unified,
still proclaim severally their own lives:
up here, stubborn on its once fortified
hill and consciously antique, Buda survives
the upstart centuries of havoc, the alien ways
of degenerate empire, equally degenerate usurper;
down there, accommodating itself to the whys
and wherefores of shifting fashion in money, architecture,
politics, and belief. Pest stands for nothing
except a certain canny ambivalence as a device
for getting by — two boroughs confronting
the world with double appearances: the human face,
and the expedient mask.

Palm Sunday: we attend
mass at the gothic church of St. Matthias
in Buda. Early-medieval chants blend
with late-medieval arches, outliving various
assaults by Turkey, the Kremlin, even and ironically
Rome; all this, Gregorian, for introit,
kyrie, gloria, and epistle, proper and ordinary.
Then, for the gospel since antiquity set
down for this date, yearly, which is
the Passion according to St. Matthew, a shift
in time: to baroque, to its first large exegesis,
by Heinrich Schütz; who paved the future, and left
his great successor signs to read, founding
the possibility of what followed, unsurpassed ever
before or since — history's supreme pairing
of faith and art. Meanwhile, this; here.
Chant-like, the narrative proceeds inexorably
through wrongful arrest, false evidence, and torture
to its inevitable end of conviction, sentence, and summary
execution: death comes, and the sung scripture
announces it; baldly, simply — "he yielded up
the ghost." Silence. A whole congregation goes
to its knees. Silence: music come to a stop.
This is not some reflex pose
of pietism: this is the intersection of history and belief;
and every one of these adamant believers

knows, somewhere in the recesses of his own life,
the taste of judicial murder, and how the murderers
are always among us. Always.

What these know,
Schütz knew in his austere day,
and Bach in his, wholly. And what they show
forth, note by devout note, is due
at least this much respect, that no one
reduce it to the mere status of artistry: this
is immensely more than just a superb contraption
of sound, this is an act of unequivocal witness;
whose rightful home is never among the arts,
but only here, within such walls and hearts.

The opening chorus of Bach's "St. Matthew Passion" summons the Daughters of Zion (and with them the whole community of the faithful) to mourn for Jesus: the Savior is spoken of as a "spotless Lamb," calling to mind the sacrificial victim of Passover, evoking the image preserved in liturgy, "Christ our Passover is sacrificed for us." Not far from Bach's church, in his time, was the Jewish quarter, where every year, with equal fidelity, the ancient Passover was commemorated. The Judenstrasse, well-known to Bach, might well have come into his thoughts at this time of sacrifice and redemption.

Judenstrasse

✸   ✸

II

Among the people here, faithful still
to ancient prescript, all homes as one
make ready the Passover: select the sacrificial
and spotless lamb, for the roast shank-bone;
set aside the egg; cleanse the plate;
gather the bitter herbs; buy the wine;
and bake the unleavened cakes, the bread they ate
in affliction — obedient: *and this shall be a sign
unto thee upon thine hand, and a memorial before
thine eyes.*

Lord, Lord of them and us,
let this season of our Passover

be for us, as for them, a righteous
sign and living memorial — a sign of trust
in our redemption, our exodus from the servitude
to sin; and a memorial of your huge cost,
paid in blood and death to make good
our huge debt — and may my humble
music serve, at least, for passing-bell.

"Herzliebster Jesu, was hast du verbrochen?" ("Beloved Jesu, how hast thou offended?") Bach's choir reflects on the guiltlessness of Christ, destined to give his life for the sins of man. This is a sacrifice commemorated by Christian choirs since antiquity — especially by monastic choirs in the Middle Ages. One of their chief rites in Holy Week was the service of Tenebrae, sung at night. In it was chanted the antiphon, "He was offered because he willed it," and the response, "Christ for us was made obedient unto death: even the death of the cross." Tenebrae factae sunt: and there was darkness over the whole land.

Tenebrae

III

To give light to them that sit in darkness
and in the shadow of death. Canticle ends, sung
from memory in the dark, the whole choir sightless:
last candle taken away from among
us, all other lights extinguished; tenebrae,
night. The heart blackens, remembering: night
there; his making ready as offertory
for us; our grievous fault. Not
yet the miracle, the tomb door thrown
on its side, the nailed foot walking forth:
now, only the dread, only the known
pain to come. Two novices, north
and south at the altar step: *Kyrie eleison;*

penitently, three times. At the choir entrance,
two juniors: *Miserere nobis;* contrition
voiced for all, in a low tone, once.
Standing in the midst, two seniors, facing
east: three versicles, in the fourth mode
solemn, of his gift and courage. Responding
the full choir: *Christ for us was made
obedient unto death.* Then, young and alone,
as he was, another novice: *Even
the death of the cross.* We kneel on stone,
silent: *Our Father who art in heaven,*
privately. *Ave Maria,* privately. Quietly
one psalm. Final prayer in the lightless
stalls, to that Lord going steadfastly
minded toward the tree. *Amen.* This
is where it begins, every year: the woman's
anointing. What he willed, now happens.

At Bethany, a woman anoints Jesus with a costly ointment. The disciples protest that the money spent on the ointment might better have been given to the poor. Jesus justifies the anointing, but reminds the disciples that "Ye have the poor always with you," in effect suggesting that one of the church's main duties should be a mission to the poor. In our time, one of the world's worst areas of poverty is Latin America. Journeying there, the poet finds himself in Brazil, in the town of Ouro Prêto — once, in Bach's day, a center of great mining wealth, now fallen into near destitution, with little to show for its former affluence but elegant baroque buildings.

Ouro Prêto

❋   ❋

I

Frozen in time, this baroque town
is all past and no future: the present
empty. Mineral wealth handed down
a vast legacy of ornate churches, giant
mansions, and grand municipal offices; all
of the one period, when empire imported Christianity,
greed, and smallpox. Later, markets fell,
exports dwindled, magnates left, and history
came to a stop. Today, the place is a museum,
the citizens almost wholly dependent on tourist
trade and whatever thin yield they can wring from
inferior soil: understandably, they lack interest

in architecture; a fine 1720 facade
makes nice photos, but you can't eat it.

The poor are always with us. Everywhere. Whose sad
plight here is seldom heeded by state
or church: governments prefer repeatedly
to rule rather than to serve; and prelates fail
grotesquely often to pause by the way and see
their neighbor Christ in the fellow-traveler who fell
among thieves, lying forsaken beside
the blind road — indifferent, the Brazilian sun
glares down, flies multiply in the lurid
wounds, and no one kneels to anoint the son
of man against his burial.

                    Outdoors, the peasants,
who know better than most the role of victim,
enact their annual passion: stark laments
bruise the air, that knit together their
pain and his in a single cry of shared
affliction; raw voices, aware that what
the world will not give them, they must accord
each other — the dues of love, the complete
gift of self.

In the adjoining room, on her old
upright, my friend plays Bach, who knew
in his day what these understand, the cold
taste of hurt, and made a language to construe
it in; and none ever, before or since,
have found an equal utterance, to speak for all
time and all our kind with the immense
charity of this music.

                    Two several
voices, merging under a deaf heaven:
linking, across huge gaps of space
and age, three April cities riven
alike with one grief — and small solace
this night, in Ouro Prêto, for him
thus readied for death: or Leipzig; or Jerusalem.

The penitential woman anointing Jesus against his burial is echoed, in Bach's music, by the Daughter of Zion grieving over the Savior's fate. Through her is sung the sorrow of all the ages, and repentance for sin: this day, in the Thomaskirche, under a late Gothic roof, and earlier, in a former church on the same site. Sorrow for the same victim, the Lamb of God that taketh away the sins of the world.

Agnus Dei

❀   ❀

II

History haunts these walls: generations
have mourned here that betrayal, that
furtive compact; here in this obedience;
before this, grieved on the same spot
in an earlier allegiance. All sorrowing, but none
absolved: each year he goes to his necessitated
death by our delivery, our treason,
and nothing changes; ransom is still paid
in blood — a young male, without blemish,
set aside for sacrifice.

III

Oh Lamb of God,
have mercy on us: thrice; for his anguish
of our making, our marring of his good.
Three times the same words: rubric
forbids this day the variant ending,
the plea for peace; mercy is all our bleak
hearts can pray for — his mercy healing
our evil: whose hour is at hand; who furled
under his wings the gross sin of the world.

Judas Iscariot plots to betray Jesus. Bach equates that betrayal with all the treacheries that mar the history of humankind. And the poet, visiting Prague not long after the Soviet treachery of 1968, sits with friends in their flat as they speak of this clandestinely, veiling what they say with recorded music, for the safety of their world.

Prague

❀ ❀

I

Music against voice: it veils the words
from the hidden microphone, blocks the quisling ear
of the not-so-secret police; in these wards,
where freedom lurks in every alley ever
ready to declare itself, the local gestapo
are a constant presence, daily visible with guns
and dogs. Therefore music, whenever the flow
of talk bucks the current of required doctrines.
And this music, in particular, is apt, grieving
over betrayal: for we speak now of an interstice
not long since, when all was spring
briefly and the tyrants ran for cover in the face
of change; whose herald and eloquent tribune met

one day, for parley, with his sworn ally
and supposed co-believer — who in fact had set
plans already to crush this silly
dream of founding here the kingdom of kindness:
not with swords and staves, but thirty-ton
tanks; and greeted him on the station platform with a kiss.
Photographed. Published in the press. My friends open
their seditious scrapbook and point, who will never forgive;
and pronounce his unpardonable name, Judas Brezhnev.

The Last Supper. Jesus institutes the Eucharist, in the holy ele-
ments of bread and wine, for all to partake of thereafter, from
that time to our own. Sacrament signifying in the breaking of
bread his body broken for the redemption of mankind, and in
the wine his blood shed. To be for ever commemorated, that
sacrifice, in the Mass. Other elements are sacred also, such as
salt and fish. But these two are especially so: the bread, and the
wine. And one of them is mentioned in the prayer he earlier
taught: our daily bread, at once the staff of life and the stuff of
salvation. In this same prayer is likewise mentioned, daily, the
coming of his Father's kingdom: the kingdom he spoke of again
at the Last Supper, when he abstained thereafter from the fruit
of the vine until that kingdom come. And all of this Bach re-
members now, remembering that night: the Last Supper; the
bread, the wine; the coming of the kingdom.

The Lord's Prayer

❀   ❀

II

Thy kingdom come . . . Daily the prayer
speaks to that future: whose coming
this covenanting word makes sure;
which all may earn who choose, who cherish among
gifts this above all, this body broken, this
blood shed for our sake, forever renewed thus
in the cup shared, the breaking of the bread.

Give us this day our daily bread . . .
Anna Magdalena bakes early, dawn
redolent twice weekly of leavened crust,
of life renewed over and over again
in its own sacraments: flour, salt, must;

fish — all central to who we are
and what we need; all, like us, his
creatures, who took here our nature
upon him and made holy all that is.

Thy will be done on earth as it is
in heaven . . . Age upon age the intent
recurs, to achieve the kingdom he promised;
and always, miserably, fails. Our bent,
perhaps, is too much and too often compromised
with self. After all, which of us,
truly, has ever prayed to have a part in
his absolute agony, his sacrifice,
and said, this night, in that garden,
Not my will but thine be done?

Gethsemane. "*Ich will bei meinem Jesu wachen*" ("I would beside my Lord be watching"). Bach, in this aria, voices his longing to keep vigil beside the Christ in this hour of his agony. As would all the faithful, whose tradition decrees, at this dark moment, that altars be stripped bare and the last service be said in a low voice with no candles lit. Whereafter they wait — for the midnight office, for the treachery to come.

Vigil

❋   ❋

III

Night watch: kneel: accept hardness,
cold: the cup will not pass from you:
this is ordained. Vow of obedience: nevertheless
not as I will: since through
man came death: accept: there is no
turning back.

        Lord, I kneel here
in this black silence: from far ago
the echo of pain rings that no prayer
can mute; and the sweat runs, clammy on brow
and hand. Mind's eye travels blind
over time to that hurt garden: below

the olives, three prone figures, unmanned
by sleep; stone's throw distant, a fourth
wakeful, mired deep in animal fear
(built in, ineluctable, since birth),
struggling up out of that near
despair onto the thin ledge of resignation.
Moon almost full, intermittently obscured
by ragged clouds: Passover eve, the preparation
(and this shall be a sign to you: deliverance assured).
Faintly visible along the ridge, a few
bare trees, stark arms mutely
reaching out for a kinder time, new
leaves: presage and remind: another tree
lifted up on another hill. Threefold
prayer. Accept. Not long now.

Mind returns. On stripped altar the veiled
cross summons: him and us. Sorrow
numbs the will. Not all endure.

Could ye not watch with me one hour?

Christ's resignation to his fate, in Gethsemane, is echoed, in Bach's score, by the chorale "Was mein Gott will" ("Oh Father, let thy will be done"). This hymn corresponds, in content and intent, to a prayer heard every year in Holy Week throughout Western Christendom, reminding the faithful of Christ's humility in the face of his impending death. And that same prayer was heard by Bach throughout his life, in all the churches he worshipped in and served. He also heard, every year at Christmas, a song to the Christ-child about a similar obedience to the Father's will, "O Jesulein süss' ("Oh sweet little Jesus"). A song about Jesus accepting in Bethlehem what he must later accept in Gethsemane, to become incarnate man and walk, in due course faithfully, through the valley of the shadow of death. And these two themes, of the Incarnation and the Passion, mingle in Bach's head, as he lies watchful in his bed on Maundy Thursday night; and the chorale tune demands a fitting harmony.

Gethsemane

❋　　❋

II

"Was mein Gott will": I lie here
in the listening dark, and the chorale tune treads
through my mind, solemn in B minor,
like a verdict: these, it proclaims, are the needs
and rewards of faith. Almost at once and seemingly
irrelevant in Holy Week, the Christmas song
"O Jesulein süss," tender lullaby
to the Child come down from on high, taking
our flesh on him at his Father's will,
for our saving. Two melodies adjacent
and parallel, each conveying what we little
expect at the time: in Bethlehem, consent
given to all that follows, as it must,

the incarnation, all the way to the cross, and sadder
music never sang infant to rest
than this, knowing the birth pang of that future;
in Gethsemane, new consent given to this
present, the hour at hand, and listen, the chorale
does not speak, as it well might, with pathos
but only with an unflinching trust — oh, tell
that truth, harmony, send that Lord
to his death with a great B major chord!

Judas Iscariot comes to Gethsemane, and with him a great multitude with swords and staves: Jesus is arrested, bound, and taken away, and the Daughters of Zion mourn for him. "Moon and stars," they lament, "have for grief the night forsaken." And here Bach images that absolute darkness suggested by the event: the taking away of Lux Mundi, the Light of the World.

At Jesus' arrest, all the disciples forsake him and flee. And Bach seizes upon that moment to conclude Part One of the score with a large movement for chorus and orchestra, depicting in brief the whole redemptive process, from the Nativity to the Passion: "O Mensch, bewein' dein' Sünde gross" ("Oh man, thy grievous sin bemoan, / For which Christ left his Father's throne, / From highest Heaven descending, / That he for us should give his blood, / Should bear our sins' o'erwhelming load, / The shameful cross enduring.")

This having been sung, there is an intermission, during which the congregation may leave the church and ponder what they have heard. And the poet, visiting Leipzig in the early 1980s, goes out with them from the Thomaskirche, Bach's church, into the chilly East German afternoon.

32

Leipzig

I

We file out of the church, his church
who made this music, his stronghold
sure: raw wind of late March
jolts the mind back from that cold,
far place to this bitter precinct
of state iron — manacles clamped daily
on the civic heart, mute badges of an extinct
freedom. Little has changed: there, crudely
hauled off in the small hours by party
goons to rigged trial and rote sentence,
a decent man was no more at liberty
then to live by the laws of his own conscience
than now and here in this city of arrests;

love subverts, love threatens disorder
in high places, love is anathema to the protectionists
of power.

        I climb the stair next door
to a dingy flat, am received like a recognition,
minds meeting across the barbed wire,
unsubmissive: somehow in this cramped den
this scholar, subsisting piecemeal on whatever
labor his hand can turn to and the commissars allow,
has carried on. He clears books apologetically
off a chair, curtains the one window
against possible surveillance, and serves coffee:
I was a stranger and he took me in. Unhesitating,
he shares his research: diagrams, records, internal
evidence in the surviving scores; everything pertaining
to how Bach probably deployed his musical
forces in the Thomaskirche, where the two
orchestras sat, and the two choirs, and the ripieno
chorus, and the soloists — the whole gigantic crew
this work requires.

        It is time to go:
we crowd back into the church again
for Part Two; ready, attuned. But before
choir and soloist, conductor, orchestra, and organ

can launch the opening movement, a local pastor
mounts the pulpit (where Luther once preached)
and briefly speaks: he bids us welcome; pays
loving tribute to Bach, who so enriched
this place and our lives; prays
for the work of the parish; bravely insists on the faith,
not the state, as the only trustworthy arbiter
of truth; and then asks us to join with
him in the Lord's Prayer. "Vater unser,"
he begins. And a thousand voices, congregated,
respond: all knowing and loving the words,
almost all born since their imported
masters first abolished goodness and afterwards
God; whose official prohibition, clearly, has never
taken effect.

      In a moment now, forlorn
and poignant, flute and oboe and violin will share
the sad burden of alto voice: to mourn
her absent Lord, taken captive, forsaken;
and the choir will ask, "Whither is thy beloved
gone, oh thou fairest among women?"
Whither then, for her, in the aching void
of that Jerusalem night? Whither annually
for Bach, remembering? Whither still, in a grieving
world under the yoke of a governing lie?

One answer, perhaps, worth heeding
is right here, in this church, these
people: in the hearts of men and women, old
and young, who yet attend these authenticities
at much risk, without despair; and are bold
to say "Our Father" here, as one,
in the Thomaskirche, this Sunday afternoon.

Jesus, having been arrested, is haled away to be tried on false charges. And Bach comments on this with the chorale "Mir hat die Welt trüglich gericht't" ("How falsely doth the world accuse"). This traditional text speaks strongly of the injustices of this world, and with confidence of God's power to mend them, to protect. Throughout the Bach Passion, the Lutheran chorales unfailingly provide a text and a melody to comment tellingly upon the events. At once simple and profound, they lie at the root of Bach's music and go to the heart of everything he believes — not only during Passiontide, but throughout the Christian year. In Advent, for instance, with "Wachet auf" ("Wake, oh wake, with tidings thrilling"). Or at Christmas, with "Vom Himmel hoch" ("From Heaven on high"). And again at Easter, with "Christ lag in Todesbanden" ("Christ lay in death's dark bonds").

Chorales

❈　　❈

II

Oh, but this music declares itself
so honestly! How it disarms! Even
prayer cannot span the great gulf
fixed between earth and far heaven
so surely as these simple tunes.
At every turn of the year, apt and sturdy,
they build their bridge; and God listens,
hearing in that cry the same humanity
he himself once shared — remembering:
and when they had sung a hymn, they went out
into the mount of Olives; then, among
the trees, sorrowful unto death, the taut
wait for betrayal; then this, this

haling off to judgment, to the verdict already
framed, the inevitable sentence.

                        Here the injustice
begins, in the accusation: and here the chorale explicitly
confronts it; not with bitterness or anger or fear;
rather and unexpectedly, with a firm and major trust
in power from above — juncture of his ear
and our voice in long mutual quest
for peace and justice. Oh, pure translation,
fusing two worlds!

                  For me, always,
here was truth's deepest repository, known
and turned to with the same instinctive immediacy as,
centuries ago, ox and ass showed,
turning rough heads towards the crib,
knowing their maker: always, from first childhood,
back there in Eisenach; and always, at the hub
of faith, these hymns spoke to man's
need and God's gift with unerring touch,
clear even to my raw perceptions
aged three. Year-long. Nonesuch.
Exact-voiced for each and every feast.

"Wachet auf," for instance: no other
herald ever proclaimed with such steadfast
nobility the high news of Advent, of our
redemption at hand. Or, at Christmas, what
can match "Vom Himmel hoch" for sheer tenderness,
serene as that great tranquil light
shining down over the sheepfold? Thus
throughout the calendar: all the way to the final
triumph of Easter, to the huge stately arc
of "Christ lag in Todesbanden"; always a chorale,
season by season of his life and work
and our saving — always: punctual, succinct.
Especially now, this holy week,
this good day: all the linked
pain and courage caught and sung, the bleak
solitude, the silence figured forth in sound;
and everywhere love, opening like a wound.

On trial, Jesus is convicted of blasphemy and pronounced worthy of death. As he stands there, he is spat upon and buffeted. This buffeting here, at the court of Caiaphas, is only a prelude to what Jesus will later undergo at the hands of the Romans: the scourging, the crown of thorns, the nailing to the cross. All of which, as Bach well understood, should cause not blame (of Jews or Romans) but remorse by the faithful, for sins committed unremittingly, that crucify him all over again every year. These are the people cited in the liturgy of Holy Week, when the Complaint of Christ is voiced in The Reproaches. In this complaint, the faithful are chided by Christ (whose words are chanted by two cantors) for their ingratitude, for their rejection of his love; all they can do in response to that rebuke is plead for mercy — this as a double choir, chanting alternately in Greek and Latin.

The Reproaches

III

Oh my people, what have I done unto thee,
or wherein have I wearied thee? Testify
against me. Two cantors, poignantly:
curved line of gentle rebuke. *I*
gave thee to drink the water of salvation:
and thou hast given me vinegar and gall.
Two choirs responding, in Greek and Latin
antiphonally: *Holy God, mighty and immortal,*
have mercy upon us.

This chant,
this reproach: almost as ancient as the paired
tongues it still utters; almost as ancient

as the offence it mourns, yearly. Nothing has altered:
we stand convicted; regret sours
in the gut. *What more could I have done
for thee that I have not done?* The fault is ours
to repent: not others'; he must atone
for us. This is the hour of our shame:
we stand, all, vested in black, guilty;
who fetched, each of us, the scourge to him,
the twined thorns; the nails; and when he was thirsty,
vinegar; the spear. Both choirs, unanimous,
in unison: *God be merciful unto us.*

Peter, having followed furtively to see the end of the trial, is himself accused by bystanders of being an accomplice of Jesus, and denies this three times, as Jesus had foretold; and the cock crows, as foretold; whereupon Peter goes out, as the text says, and weeps bitterly. And Bach sets this passage to music of heart-rending poignancy.

For all Christians, this passage is a spur to their own consciences to consider how many times they themselves have denied Christ, in ways both large and small, with much less excuse than Peter (whose very life was at risk) — prompted, far too often, by shabby meannesses of spirit. This, for them, is always a matter for grief. And if there is also ground for hope, it consists in this: Peter was forgiven, moved on to sanctity, and this can be true for them.

Their hope, however, is sometimes eroded with doubt when they consider the record of the church itself, since the church has far too often concerned itself more with gold than with good, more with power than with love. Seated in St. Peter's, Rome, the poet thinks upon these things.

Rome

I

This church, thick with gold and self,
parades before the whole world a colossal
ambiguity: half, unabashed grandeur; and half,
enduring monument to his abject denial
whose name it bears. Recall: bitter air
in the forecourt; someone had lit a fire; he warmed
himself; others nearby, accusing; fear
rank in the throat, retching up the deformed
cud of disavowal; three times; and then
the crowing of the cock. How can that degrading
hour and this magnificence, this bastion
of power, agree? Only, perhaps, by taking
the edifice, quite literally, at face value:

if it says, as indeed it does,
that buildings matter more than people, who
can dispute that so saying the place denies
its founder's teaching? Or who wonder that thousands
nowadays, hearing unmistakable the far denouncing
cry of the dispossessed, withdraw their chilled hands
from the provided warmth, the easy refuge, renouncing
its failure and theirs, and stumble blindly
out into the dark, weeping bitterly?

Jesus is taken to stand trial before Pontius Pilate, the Roman governor. Examined there, he answers nothing, facing an unjust authority with silence, as prophesied.

Silence. Bach's life was largely given to the sound of faith, at least outwardly: all those cantatas, the organ works, the B Minor Mass, the Passions, the chorales — they are a giant monument of faith made audible. To such a man, the idea of silence would seem to be alien, incongruous. Yet this is not so. In the deepest part of his being, he senses in silence something beyond even the reach of music: that remote and private place where, in utter nakedness, the soul can meet its God.

Silence

❋   ❋

II

Silence falls on the ear, enter the mind:
first, all sound muted, the clamor,
the small intrusive noises, all deadened
to make room for music, that sure
focus on things transcendental, beyond rationality
or language; then, after music, the final
note dying away, become history,
silence — and oh, to begin with, how we fill
it up with the habit of words, unvoiced but hasty,
fearing the void! Until, at last, even
that reflex verbiage, although merely
thought, falters and gives up. Then,
and only then, the real silence: we find

ourselves alone, stripped, empty, waiting
in limitless space, outside time; can stand
there attuned, on God's doorstep, listening,
unafraid.

       Lord, is this what it was
you carried everywhere with you? Even in a crowd,
this silence? This connection? Always
and absolute? Even now, before shrewd
Pilate, facing execution? Well, it was all
foretold: *He was afflicted, yet he opened not
his mouth.* Jesu, master of silence, instil
in me some small portion of that
stillness. While I live. And let me come,
in death, soundless into your kingdom.

Pilate releases Barabbas and condemns Jesus to be crucified. For Bach, the cross is a cause of reverence and of gratitude: it is for the redemption of mankind. For others later, in a largely post-Christian world, the cross is recognized as having been, too often, the occasion of other and less admirable things — not least, the oppression of the Jews. And this not only in the medieval persecutions, not only in the subsequent pogroms, but also (and most extremely) in our own time, in the Holocaust. Moreover, these cruelties have not been only elsewhere: They have been here, in our own land. Wherever the church has been, there has also been the suffering Jew. And the poet, visiting Poland in 1981, remembers this.

Warsaw

❋   ❋

I

Magnificent on the high altar in this patron
church of Solidarity, the cross proclaims pure
contradiction: at once, a sign of shame and a token
of pride; his humiliation, and our addiction to power
and wealth. Constant paradox: this same
ecclesia, with its long record of cynical aid
to kings and other tycoons in fixing fearsome
penalties for all who dare preach the creed
of liberation and love, today confronts the state
on their behalf; and finds in Christ's Passion
a metaphor to deplore and sanctify the nailed fate
of all victims, here or elsewhere, of oppression.

Irony adds itself: I go out
respectful, into the police-infested streets,
and walk around the corner and down the sunlit
boulevard, a pilgrim, to where reconstruction meets
the waste land, which once was the ghetto;
and here, sick at heart, remember how
this atrocity was prompted far ago
by blame for Golgotha from the very body that now
denounces all such crimes. Guilt
by association: "His blood be on us
and on our children": gas-ovens built
on that text are only the last ruinous
outbreak in a long plague-line of persecution
and pogrom; but no one ever heard the executioners
(those fine upstanding Christian gentlemen)
come right out and say to the governors
at the world's court, "Their blood be
on us and on our children."

                    Bach rings
in my ears, who set those words vividly
to music for double chorus, wind, and strings:
who, being a just man, might
perhaps have preferred to omit them except
that modesty forbade him to edit holy writ;
at least, though, in his own person, he kept

aloof from laying blame for the cross at the door
of innocent scapegoats — for that burden he acknowledged
himself accountable, only himself; and in score
after score, guilt racked and grief ravaged
his heart.

      Which one of us, when blame
comes to be added up, can say the same?

Jesus is mocked and struck by the Roman soldiers, who make a crown of thorns and place it upon his head. And Bach responds with the great chorale "O Haupt voll Blut und Wunden" ("Oh sacred head sore wounded"). Then Jesus is led away to be crucified, and along the way, Simon of Cyrene is conscripted to help carry the cross.

In Bach's time, and before and since, that journey was commemorated during Holy Week in the liturgy of the Stations of the Cross. In it, the faithful process around the church, stopping at the fourteen places where pictures or carvings reverently depict the incidents of Christ's Passion, from the condemnation to the entombment. At each of them a short devotion is made. These depictions have been wrought, in many places, by visual artists as accomplished, in their medium, as Bach was in music. In other places, they have been more homely and humble, the work of artisans. At either level, though, they have expressed vividly the human pain Christ had to undergo. Fourteen stations. The fifth one now: the conscribing of Simon of Cyrene.

The Stations of the Cross

✳   ✳

III

All this week, annually, the Stations:
step by step, the rehearsal: of what was done,
will be done: we tread, as he trod, the stones
of grief, the dolorous way, one by one:
leading, the processional cross, arms veiled
in purple, crucifer robed in black: following,
the priest, also black, book held
open to sad text: then, answering
sadly together, each of us. Versicle:
We adore thee, oh Christ, and we bless thee.
Lone voice hollow in bleak aisle,
echoing year after year the same misery
repeated. And our response, always the same:

Because by thy holy cross thou hast redeemed
the world.

      Crucifer kneels, for the fifth time:
priest kneels: all kneel: framed
on the north wall, Simon of Cyrene stands
to his lucky work, there by chance, whose lot
it was to share this, bear in his hands
half the load — and which of us would not
gladly take his place, were we there?

Between stations, the Stabat Mater, verse
by verse, chanted: lament for Christ's mother,
whose sorrow is like ours, only worse:
music without pretense, each syllable
granted a mere single stark note,
wrung out of some scarcely imaginable
core of anguish into this pure concentrate
of sound: fifth stanza: out of the deep,
consider well: *Who would not weep?*

Jesus comes to Calvary, and is crucified. Bach, at this moment, imagines himself among those who sat down and watched him there. He thinks of the Savior, once again, as the Light of the World, and he finds another chorale to enshrine that thought, reverencing Jesus as he undertakes now, for our sake, to enter the darkness of death. It is a moment of great poignancy at any time, but especially so in times of war, when all that's good seems to be at the mercy of evil. And modern war, with its immense power of devastation, makes that all the more true. Many of us today have lived through such a time. It is a sure sign of hope for the human spirit that in the very darkest hour of World War II the first large-scale recording ever of "The St. Matthew Passion" was made in Germany, in Leipzig, with distinguished soloists (notably Karl Erb, the foremost Bach Evangelist of modern times), the Gewandhaus Orchestra, and the choir of Bach's own church, the Thomaskirche. And in the same period, a performance of "The St. Matthew Passion" in blitzed London had similar weight. It was attended by the poet, as a young man.

London

❊   ❊

I

This is a place of skulls: laid bare
under bombs, the littered bones of history
attest: here the first huts were;
there the villas, the garrison; later, successively
imposed, the cults of wood, stone, brick,
concrete — all variously reduced by damp,
abandonment, fire, new fashions of civic
pride, or war: whose latest survivors camp
among the ruins or underground, and struggle somehow
to get on with their lives; a victim people
nailed to a fate they neither earned nor show
any wish for, but simply endure with dull
unremitting courage.

Thousands die: scraps
of flesh, bone-splinters, gouts of blood
mingle with dust and rubble — with odd outcrops:
here an ownerless arm, there a nude
staircase leading up to a vanished floor,
and sometimes, astoundingly, between voids an entire
house standing intact, complete with proprietor
setting down punctually by snug fire
a saucer of rationed milk for the family cat;
this is a landscape of contradictions.

These days,
death drops in, street by street,
random and ubiquitous: a whole neighborhood dies
at one blow; men, women, children;
civilian and military alike. And yet,
life persists, holding on to routine:
there are still jobs to go to, meals to eat,
regular family duties, functions to attend;
not least this annual St. Matthew,
unrevoked by war — and that sheer blind
insistence on it, despite the blitz, is true
promise of good overcoming finally the powers
of darkness; which, at root, this work
and his crucifixion are all about.

Wars

end, this day will pass, the dark
at noon lift; peace and resurrection will happen.
Meanwhile, I stash the shovel I work with clearing
debris from bomb sites in Bethnal Green,
homes once, and journey across intervening
time and distance, by tube, to Bach and Calvary:
and hear, oh apt to this town and year,
sung by Kathleen Ferrier, of any century
the supreme contralto, eternal woe: the Daughter
of Zion grieving at the place of skulls; her Golgotha
and ours — "Ah Golgotha! Unhappy Golgotha!"

"Ah Golgotha! Unhappy Golgotha!" Thus the Daughter of Zion grieves over Golgotha, but also goes on to proclaim the ransom of the world made sure upon a gibbet. That sacrifice prompted, from earliest times, a widespread veneration of the cross: it became ritualized, and the rite contains a Latin hymn that begins "Faithful cross, above all other / One and only noble tree." This image of cross as tree is an ancient and potent metaphor, as valid in the Reformed churches as in the Roman. Valid also for Bach, who sits at a window and contemplates a large tree behind his house, and remembers.

The Tree

❀   ❀

II

Bare in the bleak end of winter,
the tree lifts its arms, rigid
in blind prayer, a mute gesture
of longing uttered against the sad
light: longing and knowledge: of time
come round again to endure,
root and branch, cold's ultimatum
without flinching; then bear
on boughs, salvant for all to see,
the effective sign, its green remedy.

The tree inherits. And who knows
what timber memory stirs

along its veins, of lineage, of agonies
elsewhere borne; of some ancestor's
harsh privilege, to carry stalwart
on shared nails, between thieves,
the embodiment of truth? Whose willed part
it was to guarantee, in death, leaves
for trees and us — for all, a belief
in restitution, in right process, in life.

I gaze through glass: regard opposite
my gaunt elm, stiff in the frozen
air, waiting: for deliverance; obdurate.
But mind's eye, this noon
of nailing, looks beyond those
limbs, to a far hill, another
tree, another year: knows
there the death of wood, bitter
in the deep grain; and heeds the hurt
within, the desolate rending at the heart.

Jesus is mocked on the cross by passersby, and only three people stand by him in his agony; but every devout Christian wishes to have been there, to add to their number. It is a wish that Bach gives voice to through his choir: "Here would I stand beside thee," they sing: "Lord, let me not depart!"

The three who did stand by the cross of Jesus, according to scripture and tradition, were his mother, his disciple St. John, and St. Mary Magdalene. To two of them, the Blessed Virgin and the Beloved Disciple, he spoke — to their pain, out of his own — as previously he spoke, at the nailing, to ask forgiveness for his executioners. These and five other utterances from the cross constitute what are called The Seven Last Words. They have been the subject, both severally and together, of devout contemplation by saints and sinners alike. For the edification of the faithful, they have been commemorated in countless paintings and much stained glass. And, in liturgy, they gave rise to a rite called "The Seven Last Words," in which seven specially composed pieces of music reflect upon the seven utterances one by one, and seven short homilies are preached on them.

The Seven Last Words

※   ※

III

Father, forgive them: limbs stretched, to receive
the nails, jaw clenched to force
out words; at prie-dieu, our hands grieve,
wincing.

       Today in Paradise: consolation sought
and given; and which of us would not gladly,
in that place, steal his mercy too?

Woman, behold thy son: she weeps to see,
and few things, there, pierce through
his heart more sharply than that sword;
or our hearts, considering.

My God, my God,
why hast thou forsaken me? Fourth word,
quoted in this hard place of blood
and solitude from Psalm twenty-two: even
in abandonment, felt now briefly, a faithfulness
somehow to a form of faith, to far heaven
remembered; for us, in woes always less,
other psalms, other words, more
fitting our condition — none of us
was ever forsaken.

I thirst: scripture
foretold this, the vinegar lifted up, acidulous
on tongue and throat, his exposure, inevitable
as weather, to yet another gratuitous cruelty;
who thirsted then, and continually since, for a little
love to quench his parched heart — and we
respond with tart gestures, daily, of indifference
and rejection.

Father, into thy hands:
earlier the forsaken word, the deep sense
of exile, and now this, at the very grounds
of his being, this trust; which liturgy requires
us, in turn, to echo nightly, at Compline,
who sentenced him, who inflict these scars

daily, the five and saving wounds — again
and again, these debts, that payment.

It is finished: oh, great cry,
last word of victim at last moment
reversing this day, making a victory!
Lord, dying so, have mercy: send
us all, at our time, a good end.

Jesus dies upon the cross; and in a majestic few bars, Bach captures the awed response of those who were there with the centurion, that "Truly this was the Son of God."

In the death of Jesus, for all Christians, there lies the promise of the Resurrection, drawing the sting of death itself. But nothing, not even that promise, can efface the actual hideousness of that death. At the hands of some painters, it has been sublimated, even sentimentalized. But at the hands of the great German realist, Grünewald, it was presented in its full horror, without any concessions to squeamishness. This visual approach corresponds closely to Bach's deeply pictorial approach to such themes: time and again he hit upon a turn of phrase or harmonization that echoed the scene he was dealing with in an almost naively literal way. And there were certain aspects of his idiom, both melodically and harmonically, that made him supremely fitted to portray both physical and spiritual pain. This capacity of his would have been especially called up by the recollection of Golgotha; and that memory would have been especially nourished by his holding, in his mind's eye, the memory of having seen Grünewald's great Crucifixion, or at least a copy of it, in a poor and austere parish church, during a Lenten journey.

Crucifixion

❀   ❀

II

Lent: a grey afternoon in the barren season:
wan light slants down from plain
glass to bare walls: all, all is in
keeping with that cross and this lone
picture, skull-stark above the altar;
flesh and stone stripped down to essential
self; inert, locked in a timeless rigor.

Consider: this is no ordinary portrayal:
custom has sugared art, elsewhere, to coat
the event in limp crust of genteel reverence,
pallid as dough, making a mere anecdote
of the real sweat and anguish, the blood, the violence

to every felt inch, the havoc: but not here:
here, nothing is glossed over; pain
contorts the entire frame from cramped finger
and riven palm to feet in iron ruin;
torn head bowed over gaunt
thorax; face, torso, limbs grimly
suffused with death, greenish hue of incipient
rot, corpse-color, rancid, sickeningly
true to the filth and stench of this charnel
hour — worse, though, beyond worst
woe of body, mind's damage, total
desolation of knowing such ill forced
upon him, uncaring, by those he lived for us.

Light dies in the withering day: sight
dwindles: but mind's eye retains this,
dour image of our good bought
with his grief: not then only,
but now and every year of his grace;
for whom, oh, let the stave cry
aloud on the callous ear with such distress
as may, sharp as love, pierce the heart
with this sword, the knowledge of his hurt!

The body of Jesus is taken down from the cross and given to Joseph of Arimathea, who inters it in his own new tomb, hewn out of the rock.

Bach, having recounted the burial of Jesus, comes now to the finale of his work, an immense movement for double chorus and double orchestra. In it the singers, on behalf of all who were there, perform extensively the rite of farewell. "Wir setzen hier," they sing: "In tears of grief, dear Lord, we leave thee: / Hearts cry to thee, oh Saviour dear: /Lie thou softly, lie softly here." And setting this text, the composer achieves a touching blend of tenderness and sorrow, carried consistently through to the very last bar, with its plangent dissonance resolving into a solemn C minor chord.

It is this final touch which inspires the poet, attending a performance in Toronto, to realize how Bach, in a single climactic bar, crystallizes at once and for ever not only the thrust of his entire score, but also and more importantly the whole meaning of the Passion.

Toronto

❀   ❀

I

Final cadence: final master-stroke
on this vast canvas. How simple
it would have been, here, merely to invoke
the laws of harmony and move, bland and unremarkable,
to the closing chord! Not Bach, though:
even now, in this concluding bar,
he does not cease to invent, to convince, to go
(as always, score after score)
in a direction at once unexpected and, in retrospect,
inevitable. Thus here: all voices,
almost all instruments arrive in locked
step at required C minor terminus,
except the flutes: long B natural
appoggiatura, major seventh dissonant against

tonic, only slowly rising to eventual
resolution — it is one last declaring, tensed
and articulate, of what at core this work
means: that even atrocity, even this
ultimate atrocity yearly wrought on the stark
hill, evens out in the end to redemptiveness,
all discord healed; and this music,
from first to final note, leads all
who hear, not only through the whole rubric
of his oblation from last seder to burial,
but also implicitly to the foretold hope brought
to pass, the empty tomb.

           Even here.
Granted, Roy Thomson Hall is not
the Thomaskirche: all is imbued with an air
of smug glitz, from plush seats to chic
lighting; the male players are garbed, absurdly,
like waiters, and the vocal soloists like
aristocratic refugees from some nineteenth-century
ballroom — in such a setting it is hard to imagine
his last cry, his yielding up the ghost,
ever being followed by a short span
of devout silence, with a thousand three-pieced
executives and minked wives gone to their knees.
Nevertheless, even here, in this grand

palais de luxe, nothing can undermine these
holy notes, while they last: they transcend
environment, force us inexorably back to a far
ridge, three witnesses grieving, and a crossed
figure gaunt against the skyline; there for
our fault and healing.

          While they last . . .
Final chord dies away to achieved
silence. Silence. Which, abruptly and atrociously,
is shattered: several hundred Torontonians, reprieved
from Calvary and Leipzig, revert to open display
of their own culture and applaud, with great gusto
and no concern at all; not for them the question
whether this gross and mindless salvo
insults the work or trivializes its real intention,
worship — not for those on stage, either:
the conductor, who failed to print a request that there be
no applause, smirks with self-evident pleasure
and bows like a hinge; soloists preen, greedy
for adulation; choirs and choirmasters lap up
acclaim. Who, lost in all that
tumult, that vile noise, can hope
to hear the still small voice, yet
insisting, this year as every year,
"Prepare, prepare: Easter begins here"?

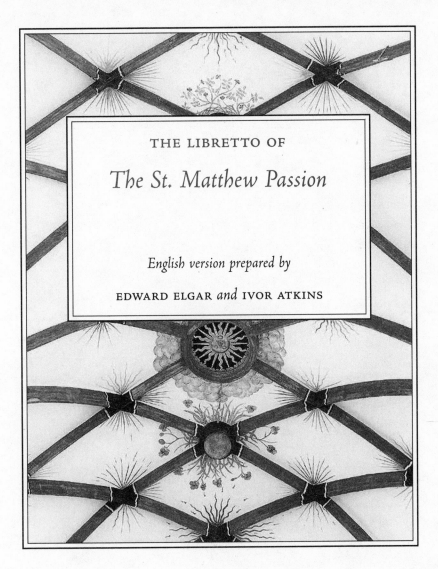

THE LIBRETTO OF

The St. Matthew Passion

English version prepared by

EDWARD ELGAR *and* **IVOR ATKINS**

Author's Note

The libretto of Bach's *St. Matthew Passion* has a structure that is at once simple and profoundly effective. The story of the Passion itself is told entirely in the words of St. Matthew's Gospel, set to music in dramatic recitatives and choruses. The passage used is Matthew 26:1–27:66, which in the libretto that follows is set in italic type. Between episodes of the story, and sometimes within episodes, are arias and arioso recitatives that reflect on the story from the standpoint of a faithful believer. The texts for these passages were furnished by the poet Picander, who in this piece rose to heights not elsewhere attained; the quality of his work, however, is not captured very well in translation in English-language performing-versions of the score because of the need to fit the syllables to the notes. Also interpolated throughout the score are traditional Lutheran chorales, harmonized by Bach. These, like the arias, reflect on the meaning of the dramatic moment to which they are juxtaposed, and, by their familiarity, they would have served in Leipzig to draw the congregation into the story of the Passion as true participants. These chorales were chosen by Bach himself, not by Picander, and in that choice, as Albert Schweitzer said, "the full depth of Bach's poetic sense is revealed." Schweitzer added, "We get the impression that he sketched the plan of the work in all its details, and that Picander worked literally under his observation. . . . The more we realize the dramatic plan of the *St. Matthew Passion* the more we are convinced that it is a masterpiece."

Part One

⁕　⁕

Come, ye daughters, share my mourning;
See Him. Whom? The Bridegroom Christ.
See Him. How? A spotless lamb.
　　O Lamb of God most holy,
　　Who on the Cross didst languish;
See it. What? His patient love.
　　O Saviour, meek and lowly,
　　Who suffered bitter anguish;
Look! Look where? On our offence.
　　The sins of man Thou bearest,
　　Our every grief thou sharest.
Look on Him. For love of us
He Himself His cross is bearing.
　　Have mercy on us, O Jesu!

79

EVANGELIST AND JESUS

When Jesus had finished all these sayings, He said unto His disciples,
Ye know that after two days is the Passover, and the Son of man shall be deliv-
ered to be crucified.

CHORALE

O blessed Jesu, how hast Thou offended,
That now on Thee such judgement hath descended?
Of what misdeed hast Thou to make confession?
Of what transgression?

EVANGELIST

Then assembled the chief priests and the scribes together, and the elders of the
people, unto the palace of the high priest, who was called Caiaphas, and con-
sulted that they might take Jesus by subtilty, and kill Him. But they said,

CHORUS

Not upon the feast day, lest haply there be an uproar among the people.

EVANGELIST

Now when Jesus was in Bethany, in the house of Simon the leper, there came
unto Him a woman, having an alabaster box of very precious ointment, and
poured it on His Head, as He sat at meat. But when His disciples saw it, they
had indignation and said,

To what purpose is this waste? For this ointment might have been sold for much, and given to the poor.

EVANGELIST AND JESUS
When Jesus understood it, He said unto them, Why trouble ye the woman? for she hath wrought a good work upon Me. For ye have the poor always with you; but Me ye have not always. For in that she hath poured this ointment on My Body, she did it to prepare Me for my burial. Verily I say to you, Wheresoever this gospel shall be preached throughout the whole world, there shall also this, that this woman hath done, be told of her for a memorial.

RECITATIVE AND ARIA: CONTRALTO
My Master and my Lord,
In vain do Thy disciples chide Thee
Because this pitying woman,
With ointment sweet, Thy Flesh
For burial maketh ready.
O grant to me, beloved Lord,
The tears wherewith my heart o'erfloweth
An unction on Thy Head may pour.

Grief for sin
Rends the guilty heart within.
May my weeping and my mourning

Be a welcome sacrifice.
Loving Saviour, hear in mercy!

Then went one of the twelve, called Judas Iscariot, to the chief priests, and said, What will ye give me, and I will deliver Him unto you? And they covenanted with him for thirty pieces of silver. And from that time he sought opportunity to betray Him.

ARIA: SOPRANO
Break in grief, Thou loving heart.
For a son whom Thou hast nourished,
Yea, a friend whom Thou hast cherished,
Gathers cruel foes around Thee,
and will like a serpent wound Thee.

EVANGELIST
Now the first day of the feast of unleavened bread, the disciples came to Jesus, saying unto Him,

CHORUS
Where wilt Thou that we prepare for Thee to eat the Passover?

EVANGELIST AND JESUS
And He said, Go ye into the city to such a man, and say unto him, The Master saith, My time is at hand, I will keep the Passover at thy house with My disci-

*ples. And the disciples did, as Jesus had appointed them, and they made ready
the Passover. Now when even was come He was sitting at meat with the
twelve. And as they did eat, He said, Verily I say to you, that one of you shall
betray Me. And they were exceeding sorrowful, and began every one of them to
say unto Him,*

CHORUS
Lord, is it I?

CHORALE
'Tis I, whose sin now binds thee,
With anguish deep surrounds Thee,
And nails Thee to the tree;
The torture Thou art feeling,
Thy patient love revealing,
'Tis I should bear it, I alone.

EVANGELIST, JESUS, JUDAS
*And He answered and said, He that dippeth his hand with Me in the dish, the
same shall betray Me. The Son of Man truly goeth as it is written of Him: but
woe unto that man by whom the Son of Man is betrayed: It had been good for
that man if he had never been born. Then answered Judas, which did betray
Him, and said, Master, is it I? He said unto him, Thou hast said. And as they
were eating, Jesus took bread, and blessed it, and brake it, and gave it to the disciples, and said, Take, eat, this is My body. And He took the cup, and gave
thanks, and gave it to them, saying, Drink ye all of it; for this is My Blood of*

the New Testament which is shed for many for the remission of sins. I say to you, I will not drink from henceforth of this fruit of the vine, until that day when I drink it new with you in my Father's kingdom.

RECITATIVE AND ARIA: SOPRANO

Although our eyes with tears o'erflow,
Since Jesus now must from us go,
His gracious promise doth the soul uplift,
His Flesh and Blood, O precious gift!
He leaves us for our souls' refreshment.
As He while in the world did love His own,
So now with love unchanging
He loves them still unto the end.

Jesus, Saviour, I am Thine,
Come and dwell my heart within.
All things else I count but loss,
Glory only in Thy Cross.
Dearer than the world beside
Is the Saviour who hath died.

EVANGELIST AND JESUS

And when they had sung an hymn, They went out into the mount of Olives. Then saith Jesus to them, All ye shall be offended because of Me this night, for it is written, I will smite the shepherd, and the sheep of the flock shall be scattered abroad. But after I am risen again, I will go before you into Galilee.

Receive me, my Redeemer,
My Shepherd, make me Thine;
Of ev'ry good the fountain,
Thou art the spring of mine.
How oft Thy words have fed me
On earth with angels' food,
How oft Thy grace hath led me
To highest Heav'nly good.

EVANGELIST, PETER, JESUS

Peter answered, and said unto Him, Though all men shall be offended because of Thee, yet will I never be offended. Jesus said to him, Verily I say unto thee, That this same night, before the cock crow, shalt thou deny Me thrice. Peter said unto Him, Yea though I should die with thee, yet will I not deny Thee. Likewise also said all the disciples.

CHORALE

Here would I stand beside Thee;
Lord, bid me not depart!
From Thee I will not sever,
Though breaks Thy loving heart.
When bitter pain shall hold Thee
In agony opprest,
Then, then will I enfold Thee
Within my loving breast.

Then cometh Jesus with them unto a place called Gethsemane, and saith to His disciples, Sit ye here, while I go yonder and pray. And He took with him Peter, and the two sons of Zebedee, and began to be sorrowful and very heavy. Then saith Jesus to them, My soul is exceeding sorrowful, even unto death: tarry ye here and watch with Me.

RECITATIVE AND ARIA: TENOR AND CHORUS

O grief! that bows the Saviour's troubled heart!
His spirit faints, His sorrow veils His face!
  My Saviour, why must all this ill befall Thee?
He to the Judgement hall is brought,
There is no help nor comfort near.
  My sin, alas! from highest Heav'n did call Thee.
The powers of darkness now assail Him,
His chosen friends will yet forsake Him.
  God took the debt from me, who should have paid it;
  On Thee he laid it.
Ah! if my love Thy stay could be,
If I could weigh Thy grief, and share it,
Could make it less, or help to bear it,
How gladly would I watch with Thee!

I would beside my Lord be watching.
  And so our sin will fall asleep.
By His Cross

I am saved from sin and loss,
His sorrows win my soul its ransom.
   The griefs that He for us endureth,
   How bitter, yet how sweet are they.

And He went a little farther, and fell on His face, and prayed, saying, O my Father, if it be possible, let this cup pass from me: yet not as I will, but as Thou wilt.

The Saviour low before His Father bending,
To gain for man by His oblation
A full salvation,
The love of God toward man commendeth.
He now will drink the cup
Unto its last and bitt'rest dregs,
Which with the sin of men is filled
And overflows.
He will not shrink,
But suffer all that God hath willed.

Gladly would I take upon me
Cross and Cup and all His burden,
Could I follow Christ my Lord.
Lo, our Lord,

In love our burden sharing,
Bears for us
The Cross with all its shame.
He has lighten'd all our sorrow.

EVANGELIST AND JESUS

And He cometh to the disciples, and findeth them asleep, and saith unto Peter, What, could ye not watch with Me one hour? Watch and pray, that ye enter not into temptation: the spirit is willing, but the flesh is weak. He went away again the second time, and prayed, saying, O my Father, if this cup may not pass away from Me, except I drink it, Thy will be done.

CHORALE

O Father, let Thy will be done,
For all things well Thou doest,
In time of need refusest none,
But helpest e'en the lowest.
In deep distress Thou still dost bless,
In wrath rememb'rest mercy;
Who trusts in Thee shall ever be
In perfect peace and safety.

EVANGELIST, JESUS, JUDAS

And He came and found them asleep again: for their eyes were very heavy. And He left them, and went away again, and prayed the third time, saying again the same words. Then cometh He to His disciples, and saith unto them,

Sleep on now, and take your rest, behold, the hour is at hand, and the Son of Man shall be betrayed into the hands of sinners. Arise, let us be going: behold, he is at hand that doth betray Me. And while He yet spake, lo, Judas, one of the twelve, came, and with him a great multitude with swords and staves from the chief priests and elders of the people. Now he that betrayed Him gave them a sign, saying, Whomsoever I shall kiss, that is he: hold Him fast. And forthwith he came to Jesus, and said, Hail Master, and kissed Him. Jesus said unto him, Friend, friend, wherefore art thou come? Then drew they near, and laid hands on Jesus, and took Him.

DUET: SOPRANO AND CONTRALTO, WITH CHORUS
Behold, my Saviour now is taken.
    Loose Him! leave Him! bind Him not!
Moon and stars
Have for grief the night forsaken,
Since my Saviour now is taken.
They lead Him hence; with cords they bind Him.

CHORUS
Have lightnings and thunders their fury forgotten?
Then open, O fathomless pit, all thy terrors!
Destroy them, o'erwhelm them, devour them, consume them with
    tumult of rage,
The treach'rous betrayer, the merciless throng.

And behold, one of them which were with Jesus, stretched out his hand, and drew his sword, and struck a servant of the high priest's, and smote off his ear. Then said Jesus unto him, Put up again thy sword into his place: for all they that take the sword, shall perish with the sword. Or thinkest thou that I cannot now pray to my Father, and He shall presently give Me more than twelve legions of angels? But how then shall the scriptures be fulfilled, that thus it must be? In that same hour said Jesus to the multitudes, Are ye come out as against a thief with swords and staves for to take Me? I sat daily among you, teaching in the temple, and ye laid no hold on Me. But all this was done, that the Scriptures of the Prophets might be fulfilled. Then all the disciples forsook Him and fled.

CHORUS

O man, thy grievous sin bemoan,
For which Christ left His Father's Throne,
From highest Heav'n descending.
Of Virgin pure and undefiled,
He here was born, our Saviour mild,
For sin to make atonement.
The dead he raised to life again,
The sick He freed from grief and pain,
Until the time appointed,
That He for us should give His Blood,
Should bear our sins' o'erwhelming load,
The shameful Cross enduring.

Part Two

❀　❀

Ah! now is my Saviour gone.
    Whither is thy beloved gone,
      O thou fairest among women?
Whither went He? I would follow.
    Whither has thy friend gone aside?
Ah! my Lamb, the slayers hold Thee.
Where now is my Saviour gone?
    For we would go with thee to seek Him.
Ah! how shall I find an answer
To assure my anxious soul?
Ah! where is my Saviour gone?

EVANGELIST

And they that had laid hold on Jesus, led Him away to the house of Caiaphas, the high priest, where the scribes and the elders were gathered together. But Peter followed Him afar off, unto the court of the high priest, and went in and sat with the servants to see the end. Now the chief priests and the elders, and all the council, sought false witness against Jesus to put Him to death, but found none.

CHORALE

How falsely doth the world accuse!
How ready justice to refuse!
How eager to condemn me!
In danger's hour,
Lord, show Thy pow'r,
From ev'ry ill defend me.

EVANGELIST, WITNESSES, HIGH PRIEST

Yea, tho' many false witnesses came, yet found they none. At the last there came two false witnesses, And said, This fellow said, I am able to destroy the temple of God, and to build it in three days. And the high priest arose, and said unto Him, Answerest Thou nothing? what is it, which these witness against Thee? But Jesus held His peace.

RECITATIVE AND ARIA: TENOR

He holds His peace, though men accuse Him falsely, that thereby He may show us how deep compassion works within Him to bear our sorrows in His heart. So we, when call'd to suffer wrong, should try to be like Him, and in affliction hold our peace.

Endure, endure!
Even lying tongues and taunting.
Suffer thou, in faith secure,
Scourge and rod,
Wait till justice of our God
Smite their hearts with sword avenging.

EVANGELIST, HIGH PRIEST, JESUS

And the high priest answered, and said unto Him, I adjure Thee by the name of the living God, that Thou tell us, whether Thou be the Christ the Son of God. And Jesus saith unto him, Thou hast said: Nevertheless I say unto you, hereafter shall ye see the Son of Man sitting on the right hand of power, and coming in the clouds of Heaven. Then the high priest rent his garments, and said, He hath spoken blasphemy: what further need have we of witnesses? behold, now ye have heard His blasphemy yourselves, what think ye? They answered and said,

CHORUS

He is worthy of death.

EVANGELIST

Then did they spit in His face, and buffeted Him, and others smote Him with the palms of their hands, and said,

Now tell us,
Thou Christ, who is he that smote Thee?

CHORALE

O Lord, who dares to smite Thee,
And falsely to indict Thee,
Deride and mock Thee so?
Thou canst not need confession,
Who knowest not transgression,
As we and all our children know.

EVANGELIST, TWO MAIDENS, PETER

Now Peter was sitting without in the court: and there came to him a damsel,
and said, Thou also wast with Jesus of Galilee. But he denied before them all,
and said, I know not what thou sayest. And when he was gone out into the
porch, another maid saw him, and said unto them that were there, This man
also was with Jesus of Nazareth, And again he denied with an oath, I do not
know the man. And after a while came to him they that stood by, and said
unto Peter,

CHORUS

Surely thou also art one of them, for thy speech bewrayeth thee.

Then began he to curse and to swear, I know not the man. And immediately the cock crew. And Peter remembered the word of Jesus, which said unto him, Before the cock crow, thou shalt deny Me thrice. And he went out, and wept bitterly.

ARIA: CONTRALTO

Have mercy, Lord, on me,
Regard my bitter weeping.
Look on me,
Heart and eyes both weep to Thee
Bitterly.

CHORALE

Lamb of God, I fall before Thee,
Humbly trusting in Thy Cross;
That alone be all my glory,
All things else I count but loss.
Jesu, all my hope and joy,
Flow from Thee, Thou sov'reign good.
Hope and love and faith and patience,
All were purchas'd by Thy Blood.

EVANGELIST AND JUDAS

Now when the morning was come, all the chief priests and elders of the people, took counsel against Jesus to put Him to death. And when they had bound

Him, They led Him away, and delivered Him to Pontius Pilate the governor.
Then Judas, which had betrayed Him, when he saw that He was condemned,
repented himself, and brought again the thirty pieces of silver to the chief priests
and elders and said, I have sinned, in that I have betrayed the innocent blood.
And they said,

CHORUS

But what is that to us? see thou to that.

EVANGELIST AND TWO PRIESTS

And he cast down the pieces of silver in the temple, and departed, and went
and hanged himself. And the chief priests took the silver pieces, and said, It is
not lawful for to put them into the treasury, because it is the price of blood.

ARIA: BASS

Give, O give me back my Lord.
See the silver, the price of blood
At your feet in horror pour'd
By the lost betrayer.

EVANGELIST, PILATE, JESUS

And they took counsel together, and bought with them the potter's field, to be a
burying place for strangers. Wherefore that field was called, The field of blood,
unto this present day. Then was fulfilled that which was spoken by Jeremy the
Prophet, saying, And they took the thirty pieces of silver, the price of Him that
was valued, whom they of the children of Israel did value; and they gave them

for the potter's field, as the Lord appointed me. Jesus stood before the governor: and the governor asked Him, and said, Art thou the King of the Jews? And Jesus said unto him, Thou sayest. And when He was accused of the chief priests and elders, He answered nothing. Then Pilate saith unto him, Hearest thou not how many things they witness against thee? And He answered him to never a word: insomuch that the governor marvelled greatly.

CHORALE

Commit thy way to Jesus,
Thy burdens and thy cares;
He from them all releases,
He all thy sorrow shares.
He gives the winds their courses,
And bounds the ocean's shore,
He suffers not temptation
To rise beyond thy pow'r.

EVANGELIST, PILATE, PILATE'S WIFE, CHORUS

Now at that feast the governor was wont to release unto the people a prisoner, whom they would. And they had at that time a notable prisoner called Barabbas. Therefore when they were gathered together, Pilate said unto them, Whom will ye that I release unto you? Barabbas, or Jesus which is called Christ? For he knew well that for envy they had delivered Him up. And while he was sitting on the judgement seat, his wife sent unto him, saying, Have thou nothing to do with that just man: for I have suffered many things this day in a dream, because of Him. But the chief priests and elders persuaded the multi-

tude that they should ask Barabbas, and destroy Jesus. The governor answered, and said unto them, Whether of the twain will ye that I release unto you? They said, Barabbas. Pilate said unto them, What then shall I do unto Jesus, which is called Christ? They all say:

CHORUS
Let Him be crucified.

CHORALE
O wond'rous love, that suffers this correction!
The Shepherd dying for his flock's protection,
The Master pays the debts His servants owe him,
And they betray Him!

EVANGELIST AND PILATE
And the governor said, Why, what evil hath He done?

RECITATIVE AND ARIA: SOPRANO
To all men Jesus good hath done:
The blind man hath He given sight,
The lame man made to walk.
He told us of His Father's word,
He cast the devils forth,
The mourners hath He comforted,
In Him a friend the sinner found.
Save good, my Jesus nought hath done.

For love my Saviour now is dying.
Of sin and guilt He knoweth nought.
So eternal desolation
And the sinner's righteous doom
Shall not rest upon my spirit.

EVANGELIST
But they cried out the more, and said,

CHORUS
Let Him be crucified.

EVANGELIST AND PILATE
When Pilate therefore saw that he prevailed nothing, but that rather a tumult was made, he took water, and washed his hands before the multitude, and said, I am innocent of the blood of this just person: see ye to it. Then answered all the people, and said,

CHORUS
His blood be on us and on our children.

EVANGELIST
Then released he Barabbas unto them: and when he had scourged Jesus, he delivered Him to be crucified.

O gracious God! Behold, the Saviour standeth bound.
They scourge Him now, and smite and wound Him!
Tormentors, stay your hands!
Are not your hearts with pity mov'd
To see such anguish meekly borne?
Ah no! your hearts are hard,
And must be like the rock itself,
Nay, more unyielding still.
Have pity! Stay your hands!

If my tears be unavailing,
Take the very heart of me.
Then, if vain be all my pleading,
When the sacred wounds are bleeding,
Let my heart a chalice be.

EVANGELIST

Then the soldiers of the governor took Jesus into the common hall, and gathered to Him The whole band of soldiers. And they stripped Him, and put on Him a scarlet robe. And they plaited a crown of thorns, and put it upon His Head, and a reed in His right Hand: and they bowed the knee before Him, and mocked Him, and said,

CHORUS

Hail, King of the Jews!

And they spit upon Him, and took the reed, and smote Him on the head.

CHORALE

O Sacred Head, surrounded
By crown of piercing thorn!
O bleeding Head, so wounded
Reviled and put to scorn!
Death's pallid hue comes o'er Thee,
The glow of life decays,
Yet angel hosts adore Thee,
And tremble as they gaze.

In this Thy bitter Passion,
Good Shepherd, think of me
With Thy most sweet compassion,
Unworthy though I be:
Beneath Thy Cross abiding,
For ever would I rest,
In Thy dear love confiding,
And with Thy presence blest.

EVANGELIST

And after that they had mocked him, they took off from him the robe, and put His own raiment on Him, and led Him away to crucify Him. And as they

came out, they found a man of Cyrene, Simon by name: him they compelled to
bear His Cross.

RECITATIVE AND ARIA: BASS
In truth, to bear the Cross our flesh and blood
Are loth to be constrained;
For that which works our chiefest good
Most hardly is attained.

Come, healing Cross,
O joy to share it!
My Saviour, lay on me its weight.
Come, healing Cross,
For me prepare it,
My Saviour, lay on me its weight.
And if the burden grow too great,
Then help Thou me, O Lord, to bear it.

EVANGELIST
And when they were come unto a place called Golgotha, that is to say, a place
of a skull, they gave Him vinegar to drink mingled with gall: and when He
had tasted thereof, He would not drink. And when they had crucified Him,
they parted His garments, and cast lots upon them, that it might be fulfilled
which was spoken by the Prophet, They parted my garments among them, and
upon my vesture did they cast lots. And sitting down, they watched Him there:
and set up over His head His accusation, written, This is Jesus the King of the

Jews. Then were there two thieves crucified with Him: one on the right hand,
and one on the left. And they that passed by, reviled Him, wagging their heads,
and saying,

CHORUS

Thou that destroyest the temple of God, and buildest it in three days, save thy-
self: If thou be the Son of God, come down from the cross.

EVANGELIST

Likewise also the chief priests mocking Him, with the scribes and elders, said,

CHORUS

He saved others; Himself He cannot save: If He be the King of Israel, let Him
now come down from the Cross, and we will believe Him. He trusted in God;
let Him deliver Him now, if He will have Him: for He hath said, I am the Son
of God.

EVANGELIST

The thieves also, which were crucified with Him, cast the same in His teeth.

RECITATIVE AND ARIA: CONTRALTO AND CHORUS

Ah, Golgotha! Unhappy Golgotha!
The Lord of Glory here
'Mid shame and scorn must perish;
The blessed Saviour of the world
Upon th'accursed Tree now hangs;

The Lord Who heaven and earth created,
Of life and light is now bereft;
The Sinless here as Sinner dieth.
Ah, how this grief doth pierce my soul!
Ah, Golgotha! Unhappy Golgotha!

See the Saviour's outstretched Hands!
He would draw us to Himself.
Come! Come where? In Jesu's bosom seek Redemption,
Seek ye mercy, seek them! Where? In Jesu's bosom.
Live ye, die ye, rest ye here,
Ye whom sin and guilt oppress,
Rest ye! Where? In Jesu's bosom.

EVANGELIST AND JESUS
*Now from the sixth hour there was darkness over all the land unto the ninth
hour. And about the ninth hour Jesus cried with a loud voice, and said, Eli, Eli,
lama sabachthani? that is to say, My God, my God, why hast Thou forsaken
Me? Some of them that stood there heard that, and said,*

CHORUS
He calleth for Elias.

EVANGELIST
*And straightway one of them ran, and took a sponge, and filled it with vinegar,
and put it on a reed, and gave Him to drink. And others said,*

Let be, let us see whether Elias will come to save Him.

Jesus, when He had cried again with a loud voice, yielded up the ghost.

CHORALE
Be near me, Lord, when dying,
O part not Thou from me!
And to my succour flying,
Come, Lord, and set me free!
And when my heart must languish
In death's last awful throe,
Release me from mine anguish,
By Thine own pain and woe.

EVANGELIST
And behold, the veil of the temple was rent in twain, from the top unto the bottom. And the earth did quake, and the rocks were rent. And the graves were opened and there arose many bodies of the saints which had slept, and coming forth from the graves after His resurrection, and went into the holy city, and appeared unto many. Now when the centurion, and they that were with him, watching Jesus, saw the earth quake, and those things that were done, they feared greatly, saying,

CHORUS

Truly this was the Son of God.

EVANGELIST

And many women were there (beholding afar off) which followed Jesus from Galilee, ministering unto Him: Among which was Mary Magdalene, and Mary the mother of James and Joses, and the mother of Zebedee's children. When the even was come, there came a rich man of Arimathaea, named Joseph, who also himself was Jesus' disciple: He went to Pilate, and begged the body of Jesus: Then Pilate commanded the body to be delivered.

RECITATIVE AND ARIA: BASS

At evening, hour of calm and peace,
Was Adam's fall made manifest;
At evening, too, the Lord's redeeming love;
At evening homeward turned the dove
And bore the olive leaf as token.
O beauteous time! O evening hour!
Our lasting peace is now with God made sure,
For Jesus hath His Cross endured.
His body sinks to rest.
Go, loving servant, ask thou it.
Go, be it thine, the lifeless Saviour's body,
O wond'rous gift! O precious, Holy burden!

Make thee clean, my heart, from sin.
Unto Jesus give thou welcome.
So within my cleansed breast
Shall He rest,
Dwelling evermore within me.
World, depart; let Jesus in!
Make thee clean, my heart, from sin.

EVANGELIST

And Joseph took the body, and wrapped it in a clean linen cloth, And laid it in his own new tomb, which he had hewn out in the rock: and he rolled a great stone to the door of the sepulchre, and went his way. And Mary Magdalene was there, and the other Mary, sitting over against the sepulchre. Now the next day that followed, the day of the preparation, the chief priests and Pharisees came together unto Pilate, and said,

CHORUS

Sir, we remember that that deceiver said, while He was yet alive, After three days I will rise again. Therefore command the grave to be made sure, until the third day, lest His disciples come by night, and steal Him away, and say unto the people, He is risen from the dead: so the last error shall be worse than the first.

EVANGELIST AND PILATE

Pilate said unto them, Ye have a watch, go your way, make it as sure as ye can. So they went, and made the sepulchre sure, sealing the stone, and setting a watch.

And now the Lord to rest is laid.
　　Lord Jesu, fare Thee well.
His task is o'er; for all our sin He hath atoned.
　　Lord Jesu, fare Thee well.
O blest and holy Body
See, with repentant tears we would bedew it,
Which our offence to such a death has brought.
　　Lord Jesu, fare Thee well.
While life shall last, O let Thy suff'rings claim our love,
Since Thou for man salvation sure hast wrought.
　　Lord Jesu, fare Thee well.

CHORUS

In tears of grief, dear Lord, we leave Thee,
Hearts cry to Thee, O Saviour dear.
Lie Thou softly here.
Rest Thy worn and bruised Body,
Lie Thou softly here.
At Thy grave, O Jesu blest,
May the sinner, worn with weeping
Comfort find in Thy dear keeping,
And the weary soul find rest.
Sleep in peace, sleep Thou in the Father's breast.